Sign up to my newsletter for updates and free downloads at www.annastylesauthor.com

Anna Styles 2019
St Helier, Jersey, CI

ISBN (paperback): 978-1-9162343-1-4
ISBN (e-book): 978-1-9162343-0-7

Text copyright: Anna Styles 2019
Illustrations: Canva

Moral rights asserted.
All rights reserved. No part of this publication may be reproduced, stored in or introduced into a retrieval system, or transmitted in any form, or by any means, (electronic, mechanical, photocopying, recording or otherwise) without the prior written permission of the author/publisher. Any person who does any unauthorised act in relation to this publication may be liable to criminal prosecution and civil claims for damages.

1 2 3 4 5 6 7 8 9 10

Like a rainbow there are lots of parts to me and I AM AMAZING just as I am.

(and this amazing
book belongs to me)

....

I am shy

I feel shy sometimes. That's ok.
Everyone feels shy or nervous sometimes.

I am thoughtful

Sometimes I like to sit quietly and
think about things. There is a lot to think about.

I am friendly

I like meeting people and making friends.

I am LOUD

I am not always loud, but sometimes I can be VERY loud, especially when I am excited or when I am playing.

I am cheerful

I am cheerful and I like spending time with people who are cheerful and positive.

I am scared

Some things are scary.
I like to feel safe.

I am happy

I love feeling happy, it feels warm and cosy inside.
I like it when other people are happy too.

I am grumpy

Sometimes I get really grumpy and lots of things make me angry and fed up. It usually passes if I work out why I am grumpy and I do something about it.

I am sad

It is ok to feel sad but it is nice to talk to someone and share how I feel, then sometimes I feel better.

I am jealous

Sometimes I feel jealous when I see people doing things
I want to do or when they have things I want to have.
It feels like there is a green-eyed monster inside me when I get jealous.

I am worried

When I am worried I think about the thing I am worrying about lots and lots. That makes me worry more. Telling someone what I am worried about often helps.

I am angry

I get so frustrated when I am angry and it is hard to calm down. I just want to shout and scream to get all the anger out. I usually feel better after a while.

I am loving

I love the special people in my life and they love me.
Thinking about people I love makes me feel warm and fuzzy.

I am embarrassed

If I am embarrassed I can go red and blush, then I feel more embarrassed. Sometimes I just feel squirmy inside.

I am uncomfortable

I feel uncomfortable sometimes when I am in situations
I do not like. It is good to tell people that I am not
feeling good and then they might be able to help me feel better.

I am stubborn

If I do not want to do something I can be very stubborn
and refuse to do it no matter what. Sometimes I miss out on doing
fun things because I do not want to change my mind.

I am excited

I get so excited sometimes when we are going to do something fun. I jump up and down and I clap my hands and I smile the biggest smile.

I am brave

When I am scared I try to work out what is making me frightened and then I can be brave and face my fears.

I am tired

I don't always know how tired I am until a big yawn sneaks up on me.
When I am tired it is good to have a rest.

I am bored

It is so boring being bored. It is good to think of something interesting to do and then I am not bored any more.

I am confused

Sometimes I don't understand what is happening around me.
I get confused and I want someone to explain things.

I am curious

I love learning new things.
I am interested in lots of things.

I am caring

I care about my friends and family. I love animals and I care about the world around me.

I am lots of things at different times.

I am like a rainbow.
There are lots of different parts to me
and they all make me the
bright and beautiful person I am.

I am
AMAZING

I am learning every day what kind of person
I want to be and I am amazing just as I am.

YOU are AMAZING just as you are.

You are UNIQUE and SPECIAL
no matter what anyone
says or does.

Be true to yourself and shine brightly.

How are you feeling?

...

Is there anything you want to talk about today?

...

What do you feel good about today?

...

Printed in Great Britain
by Amazon